WHAT'S ON MyPlate?

HEALTHY SNACKS On MyPlate

by Mari Schuh

Consulting editor: Gail Saunders-Smith, PhD

Consultant: Barbara J. Rolls, PhD
Guthrie Chair in Nutrition
Pennsylvania State University
University Park, Pennsylvania

CAPSTONE PRESS
a capstone imprint

Pebble Plus is published by Capstone Press,
1710 Roe Crest Drive, North Mankato, MN 56003
www.capstonepub.com

Library of Congress Cataloging-in-Publication Data
Schuh, Mari C., 1975–
Healthy snacks on MyPlate / by Mari Schuh.
    p. cm.—(Pebble plus. What's on my plate?)
  Includes bibliographical references and index.
  Summary: "Simple text and photos describe USDA's MyPlate tool and its healthy snack choices for children"—Provided by publisher.
ISBN 978-1-4296-8748-5 (library binding)
ISBN 978-1-4296-9418-6 (paperback)
ISBN 978-1-62065-328-9 (eBook PDF)
 1. Snack foods—Juvenile literature. 2. Nutrition—Juvenile literature. I. Title.
TX740.S32573 2013
664'.6—dc23   2012011318

Information in this book supports the U.S. Department of Agriculture's MyPlate food guidance system found at www.choosemyplate.gov. Food amounts listed in this book are based on daily recommendations for children ages 4-8. The amounts listed in this book are appropriate for children who get less than 30 minutes a day of moderate physical activity, beyond normal daily activities. Children who are more physically active may be able to eat more while staying within calorie needs. The U.S. Department of Agriculture (USDA) does not endorse any products, services, or organizations.

Editorial Credits
Jeni Wittrock, editor; Gene Bentdahl, designer; Svetlana Zhurkin, media researcher; Kathy McColley, production specialist; Sarah Schuette, photo stylist; Marcy Morin, studio scheduler

Photo Credits
All photos by Capstone Studio/Karon Dubke except:
Shutterstock: Robyn Mackenzie, back cover, Svetlana Lukienko, cover; USDA, cover (inset), 7

Note to Parents and Teachers

The What's on MyPlate? series supports national science standards related to health and nutrition. This book describes and illustrates healthy snacks, as recommended by the USDA's MyPlate guidelines. The images support early readers in understanding the text. The repetition of words and phrases helps early readers learn new words. This book also introduces early readers to subject-specific vocabulary words, which are defined in the Glossary section. Early readers may need assistance to read some words and to use the Table of Contents, Glossary, Read More, Internet Sites, and Index sections of the book.

Printed and bound in China. PO5151

Table
of Contents

Tasty Snacks

A snack is a small amount
of food you eat between meals.
The right snacks give you
energy until your next meal.

4

MyPlate

MyPlate is a tool that
helps you eat well.
MyPlate shows you how
to choose healthy foods.

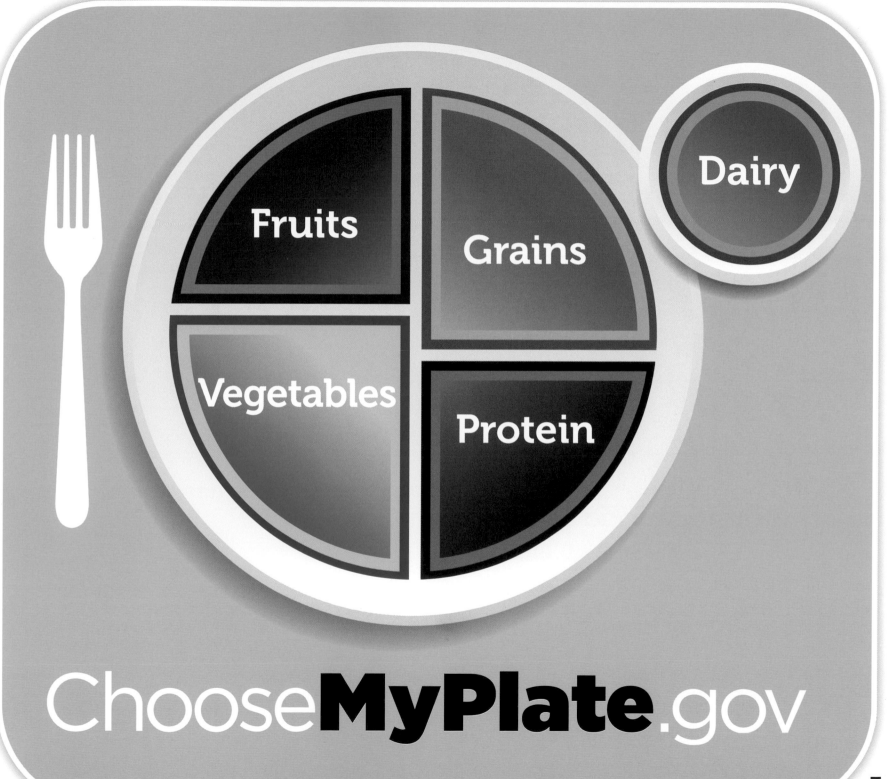

Fruits

Grains

Dairy

Vegetables

Protein

ChooseMyPlate.gov

You can choose small snacks from every food group. Try to eat snacks made from two or more food groups.

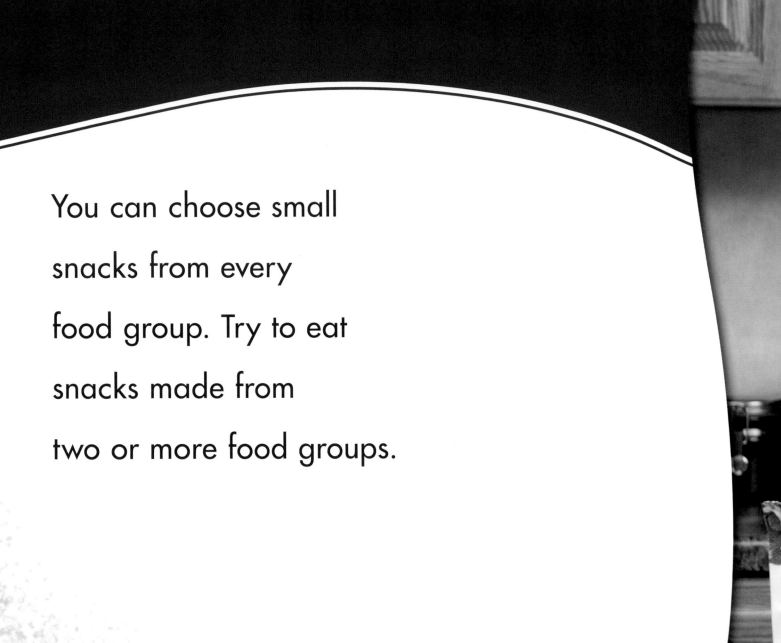

8

Snack Time

The best snacks taste good and are good for you. Graham crackers dipped in yogurt are a healthful, yummy choice!

Can't wait until lunch?
A small peanut butter
and banana sandwich
will keep you going
until your next meal.

Rumble, rumble.

Is your stomach growling?

Make your own snack mix.

Choose cereal, nuts, seeds,

and dried fruit.

14

Munch on crunchy
veggies with low-fat
dip or salad dressing.
How many colors
can you eat?

In a rush? Fruit is

a quick, healthy snack

that's easy to pack.

Grab an apple and go!

Keep your body

fueled for fun.

What are your favorite

healthy snacks?

Tasty Snack Ideas

If you have the munchies between meals, eat a small, healthy snack. Small snacks will fuel your body until your next meal.

carrots and low-fat dip

orange slices

½ cup (120 mL) cherry tomatoes

cereal with fruit

½ ounce (15 grams) sunflower seeds

low-fat cheese and whole grain crackers

mini rice cakes

sliced lean chicken with low-fat cheese

dried apricots

Glossary

energy—the strength to be active without getting tired

food group—one of the six different categories of foods people need, including dairy, fruit, grain, protein, sugars and fats, and vegetable

fuel—to give energy

MyPlate—a food plan that reminds people to eat healthful food and be active; MyPlate was created by the U.S. Department of Agriculture

snack—a small amount of food people eat between meals

Read More

Borgert-Spaniol, Megan. *Healthy Eating.* Eating Right with MyPlate. Minneapolis: Bellwether Media, 2012.

Lee, Sally. *Healthy Snacks, Healthy You!* MyPlate and Healthy Eating. Mankato, Minn.: Capstone Press, 2012.

Rockwell, Lizzy. *Good Enough to Eat: A Kid's Guide to Food and Nutrition.* New York: HarperCollins Publishers, 2009.

Internet Sites

FactHound offers a safe, fun way to find Internet sites related to this book. All of the sites on FactHound have been researched by our staff.

Here's all you do:

Visit *www.facthound.com*

Type in this code: 9781429687485

 **Super-cool stuff!** Check out projects, games and lots more at **www.capstonekids.com**

Index

dairy, 10

energy, 4

favorite snacks, 20

food groups, 8

fruit, 12, 14, 18

grains, 10, 14

low-fat, 16

MyPlate, 6

snack sizes, 4, 8, 22

vegetables, 16

Word Count: 163
Grade: 1
Early-Intervention Level: 15